THE 13TH COMMANDMENT

the 13th COMMANDMENT

by

Frances B. Lancaster

The 13th Commandment
By Frances B. Lancaster

Quotes are from A Course In Miracles.
The workbook lesson number is stated.
Other quotes are from the 2nd edition of the text.
Images taken from *Picture Puzzles or How to Read the Bible by Symbols,* Frank Beard et al., J. L. Nichols & Co., 1903

© Frances Lancaster 2013
Edited by Ruth L. Miller, Ph.D. and Noel McInnis, Ph.D.
Managing Editor: Michael Terranova

ISBN: 978-0-945385-84-4

WiseWoman Press
Vancouver, WA 98665

www.wisewomanpress.com
pra4all@comcast.net

Image symbolizing "I Am Being Loved By God"
created by Marlene King

Dedicated to:
those who have
opened my
heart
to
love...

Thank You!

Special gratitude to Rev. Dr. Noel McInnis, Ph.D. and Rev. Dr. Ruth L. Miller, Ph.D. for their editing skills and guidance in preparing this manuscript.

FOREWORD

This is a book to grow on – though only as you first allow this book to grow on you.

Seldom has so much been said in so few words, which thereby places an obligation on readers of these words to take the time required to savor their rich flavoring.

A superficial reading of these pages can lead to a false conclusion that "I've heard this all before," when the more accurate conclusion may be, "I've *seen* this all before." If actually hearing what is signified by this book's words was already a common experience, there would be no point in their presentation for us to be seeing them here.

Never has there been a more appropriate time to truly hear these words, and the author has prescribed how best to mindfully read them for the hearing that both her words and their readers deserve. We will do well to take her prescription for our savoring of their flavor.

A Quaker proverb proclaims that "To listen a soul into disclosure and discovery is the greatest service one human being can offer another." This book offers a do-it-yourself opportunity for self-disclosing and discovering our own souls.

~ Rev. Noel McInnis

PREFACE

After reading Eben Alexander's book, Proof of Heaven, I began contemplating the idea of what it means to have the awareness of "being loved by God." He tells us his experience of "Heaven" showed him that:

- You are loved and cherished, dearly, forever.

- You have nothing to fear.

- There is nothing you can do wrong

I wondered how many of us really have a tangible feeling of being cherished and loved by God? Certainly we have been told to love God, but what about the reciprocal aspect?

Consider the

how

they

grow;

they

not, neither do they

and

yet

I

say

unto

you

that

in all his glory was not arrayed like one of these.

LUKE xii, 27.

X

How many of us know, really *know,* that we neither have to toil nor spin to have what we need—that our awareness of God's Love for us is sufficient to supply all our needs?

BE COMFORTED AND FEEL THE
HOLY SPIRIT
WATCHING OVER YOU IN
LOVE AND PERFECT CONFIDENCE
IN WHAT HE SEES.

T.436

Perhaps it's a "given" in some circles, but wouldn't fully embracing this idea be a gateway to genuine freedom? Would it close the gap of seeming separation that motivates us to look for "love" in all kinds of ways in the outer world? Would embracing this feeling shift our mode of operation from desperation, based on appearances, to inspiration from the Spirit of love within? I believe this is a key factor in bringing greater peace to the world.

This book is short and one might be tempted to read it all at once. I believe the greater benefit will come as it is read and reflected upon. I encourage you to spend a few minutes in quiet reflection as guided.

REST IN HIS LOVE
AND PROTECT YOUR REST
BY LOVING.

T. 128

SUGGESTIONS FOR USING THIS BOOK

The quotes and reference pages you see come from a document of over 1200 pages that reflect a very high state of unity consciousness. To live from its wisdom has been my purpose for the past 33 years. Its words have brought peace to my mind and joy to my heart. You can do a web-search on *A Course in Miracles* to find out more about this sacred text.

My suggestion would be to read the first 13 pages of text, and put the book down and meditate on what has been shared. Where have you been nudged by God into an exciting new idea – then been talked out of it?

Proceed the next day with 6 more pages (14-19). Do we always remember that what we see has come from the invisible? Do we really know that our true essence is spiritual?

Continue on another day with (20-27). To shift our consciousness takes effort and willingness. Are we beginning to contemplate the value of this shift?

Next, read (28-35). In what ways can you cultivate this awareness at a deeper level?

Next (36-41). What is your experience with the "still small voice?" Is it still difficult to determine whether it is ego (voice of the past and fear) or the Voice for Love? We can experiment with small things when asking for guidance. Our certainty grows with experience and practice.

Next, (42-47). Self reflection is very important to our spiritual growth. It is said that awareness is curative. Without knowing our blind spots, how can we bring about change?

Next (48-51) Do you think it is possible to find peace at any chosen moment? Why not be on the "look out" today for opportunities to choose peace?

Next (52-57). How can this feeling bring greater abundance? Do you think it is possible?

Next (58-63). How do you rate your sense of joy on a scale of 1 to 10, 10 being the highest? Joy is the unmistakable experience of God's presence.

Next (64-67). What "conventional wisdoms" are you hanging on to? Is the world missing your unique contributions? Are you willing to share?

Next (68-77). Choosing a quiet time of reflection makes a significant impact on our ability to choose peace in the daily activities that confront us. Early in the morning is a good time to begin with gratitude, prayer and reflection.

Lastly (78-87). Can we begin to look on all things with love instead of the judgment we have perhaps practiced in the past? We are told to be the change we want to see. We really do make a difference in this world, and practicing the 13th Commandment is a good way to get started.

IN QUIETNESS ARE ALL THINGS
ANSWERED, AND IS EVERY
PROBLEM QUIETLY RESOLVED.

T.574

A SON (CHILD) OF GOD
IS HAPPY ONLY WHEN
HE KNOWS
HE IS WITH GOD.

T.136

THE THIRTEENTH
COMMANDMENT

"NURTURE
THE AWARENESS
OF BEING LOVED BY GOD"

It is time for a New Commandment, one that embraces all the others and places our awareness squarely on the Truth that lives within us.

This Commandment can bring peace to the world! But first, it will bring peace to your own heart.

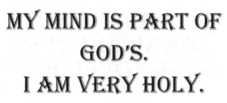

MY MIND IS PART OF GOD'S.
I AM VERY HOLY.

WB Lesson 35

My husband built a beautiful gate with a large circle in the middle. It frames a lovely spot in our garden, and a metal statue of a blue heron peaks out from behind the circle. The gate exists because of The Thirteenth Commandment. I'm sure my husband didn't realize this. He was just doing what comes naturally. He was responding to being loved by God.

God is always in the process of loving us by giving us ideas These ideas inspire us to extend qualities we associate with our Creator; love, peace, joy, harmony, beauty, abundance, etc. Most of the time, however, most of us ignore these promptings.

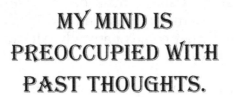

MY MIND IS PREOCCUPIED WITH PAST THOUGHTS.

WB Lesson 8

We do this because there is another voice that domi-nates our human experience. It tells us why we should be afraid to express these ideas. Perhaps there is too much work involved. It tells us about all the pitfalls that could happen. "Watch out! You'll make a mistake," it says. The moment of great inspiration from our Source slips away unnoticed. Our purpose fades into the background of the noise in the world.

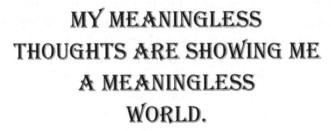

MY MEANINGLESS
THOUGHTS ARE SHOWING ME
A MEANINGLESS
WORLD.

WB Lesson 11

We are bereft of what is called a Holy Instant, a time in which we could have bathed in an intimate experience of our Creator's love and joy. In the emptiness, we feel disconnected from life itself and attempt to fill the gap with meaningless activities.

GOD BEING LOVE, IS ALSO HAPPINESS.

WB Lesson 103

Many of these turn out to be addictions. We give our inner power away to outside influences. One more trip to the mall, another hour surfing the internet or TV channels, or more dangerous, drugs and alcohol, all choices we think will make us feel better.

They might give us a momentary "high," but the real "high" has its source right within our divine inheritance.

God is love, we've been told. In the Bible, Jesus tell us that loving God and loving our neighbor as ourselves is the best guideline for living a happy life.

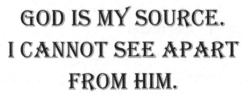

GOD IS MY SOURCE.
I CANNOT SEE APART
FROM HIM.

WB Lesson 43

We can begin to practice the first part of his advice through our acts of appreciation. When we see something beautiful we can start connecting this beauty with its source, God. When we observe a room full of happy children at play, we can recognize that God is showing up as joy. Listening to a favorite piece of music, we become aware that we are emotionally stirred. Perhaps we are noticing a sense of peace, a feeling of love or are uplifted by the rhythm. In gratitude, we praise God for these gifts.

As we gaze at the pounding ocean waves or a thunder storm, we stand in awe at the power of God. When we view an act of human kindness, our realization of God's compassion becomes apparent.

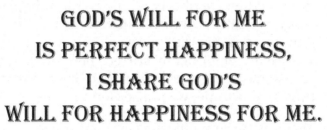

GOD'S WILL FOR ME
IS PERFECT HAPPINESS,
I SHARE GOD'S
WILL FOR HAPPINESS FOR ME.

WB Lessons 101, 102

We marvel at nature's bounty and associate God's goodness with abundance.

In these moments, we find it easy to say, "I love God," and thus follow the advice of Jesus. Not everyone pays attention and makes the connection, however.

The flow of appreciation begins with us, but the magic happens when we become aware that these experiences which initiate the feeling that *we love God* are also the same experiences that help us understand how much *we are loved by God*. The circle is complete. We have moved away from our sense of separation from God to "knowing" our oneness.

GOD GAVE THE HOLY SPIRIT
TO YOU, AND GAVE HIM THE
MISSION
TO REMOVE ALL DOUBT
AND EVERY TRACE OF GUILT THAT
HIS DEAR SON (CHILD)
HAS LAID UPON
HIMSELF

T.267

We are not alone in existing in this three dimensional life. Just because we can't see the Presence of Love with our eyes, doesn't mean it is not there. Our physical eyes are so accustomed to thinking our reality is limited by forms and interactions; we have forgotten that everything visible begins in the invisible.

I GAVE ONLY
LOVE TO THE KINGDOM
BECAUSE I BELIEVED THAT WAS
WHAT I WAS. WHAT YOU
BELIEVE YOU ARE
DETERMINES
YOUR
GIFTS.

T.113

We have been told many times that we are Spirit, but in living out that Reality, we let the appearances of our world and the world in general deceive us. Our Spiritual body is unlimited and joined with the Love of eternity. It is without form; we can let go of the idea of bodies when it comes to thinking of our possibilities of bringing love into expression.

SPIRIT
IS IN A STATE OF
GRACE FOREVER.
YOUR REALITY IS ONLY SPIRIT.
THEREFORE YOU ARE
IN A STATE
OF GRACE
FOREVER.

T.10

This is the great shift we are being asked to make in practicing the Thirteenth Commandment. All is not felt, touched, heard, seen, nor tasted with our physical senses. They serve us well within the limitations of our physical form, but beyond the information our senses tell us is a whole realm of thought that supersedes the physical.

YOU HAVE THE RIGHT
TO ALL THE UNIVERSE;
TO PERFECT PEACE,
COMPLETE DELIVERANCE FROM
ALL EFFECTS OF SIN, AND TO THE
LIFE ETERNAL,
JOYOUS AND COMPLETE
IN EVERY WAY,
AS GOD APPOINTED FOR
HIS HOLY SON (CHILD).

T.538

To move from an "idea" into practical application requires willingness to step more fully into the unknown, so
that it can be brought into the known. It is like gathering
the bricks necessary to build a home. As we gather the
bricks, we are able to begin the foundation building.

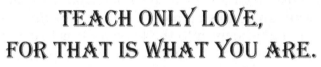

TEACH ONLY LOVE,
FOR THAT IS WHAT YOU ARE.

T.94

Cultivating our awareness of being loved by God is about building the foundation of a spiritual life in consciousness. We gather ideas that guide our thinking in a new way. The insights we gather as we begin to feel God's love for us creates a new being, us. We are changed at depth. Our lives flow from a fountain of love and selflessness. We are the hands and feet of our Creator.

YOUR TASK IS NOT TO SEEK
FOR LOVE, BUT MERELY TO SEEK
AND FIND ALL OF THE BARRIERS
WITHIN
YOURSELF THAT YOU HAVE
BUILT AGAINST IT.

T.338
Also attributed to Rumi.

God is Love, we are told in the Bible. It also tells us we are made in the image of God. That must mean we are Love. The Bible states that Moses was given The Ten Commandments to guide our lives in living according to Love or how to express this love out into the world.

"IT IS IN THE REALITY OF NOW,
WITHOUT PAST OR FUTURE
THAT THE BEGINNING OF THE
APPRECIATION OF ETERNITY
LIES."
T24

To reiterate, Jesus condensed these into what is called his Two Commandments; "Love the Lord thy God with all your heart and soul and mind and strength, and Love your neighbor as yourself." All of these Commandments are about extending the Love that we are.

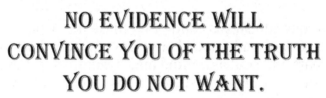

NO EVIDENCE WILL
CONVINCE YOU OF THE TRUTH
YOU DO NOT WANT.

T.333

This is the first problem. Do most of us relate to the idea that we are Love? Has our history and personal experience diverted us from this awareness? Aren't we more aware of our faults, our mistakes, our short comings than the Truth about ourselves? Do we even question and ponder the idea that perhaps we are more than the life situations we have been involved in? Are we more inclined to wait for inner reflection until we have crashed against trauma and finally recognize there must be a better way?

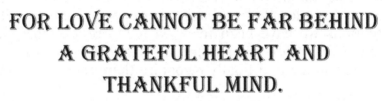

FOR LOVE CANNOT BE FAR BEHIND
A GRATEFUL HEART AND
THANKFUL MIND.

M.58

Even if we are generous and sharing of our personal wealth, even if we are grateful for our abundance of life's good, have we really thought much about the idea that, "God loves us?" It would seem obvious to believe this, but why not ask yourself, "Do I really *feel* loved by God?"

WHEN YOU HAVE LEARNED
HOW TO DECIDE WITH GOD,
ALL DECISIONS BECOME
AS EASY AND
AS RIGHT AS BREATHING.
THERE IS NO
EFFORT, AND YOU WILL BE
LED AS GENTLY
AS IF YOU WERE BEING CARRIED
DOWN A QUIET PATH
IN SUMMER.

T.280

It's one thing to extend goodness outward as prompted by an invisible Presence within ourselves. All of us have been touched by this experience and have followed through. We may have even noticed that as we have shared some form of "goodness," we have been given a gift as well.

In Truth, giving and receiving are the same. There is a certain joy that spills over us as a good deed is accomplished. At a deeper level, our oneness with all creation has been felt.

THE HOLIEST OF ALL THE SPOTS
ON EARTH IS WHERE AN ANCIENT
HATRED HAS BECOME
A PRESENT LOVE.

T.562

Traveling the universe is a mighty task for us humans. Blinded by past assumptions, we miss the golden opportunities to exist in the awareness of our True nature, Love.

What would it take for us to raise our consciousness to live in the awareness of Love?

IT IS QUITE POSSIBLE TO REACH GOD.
IN FACT, IT IS VERY EASY,
BECAUSE IT IS THE
MOST NATURAL
THING IN
THE WORLD.

M.78

First of all, we must begin to understand that being created as Love means that we have a guidance system, which, when followed, will lead us in the direction of harmonizing conflict and returning our emotional/mental states to peace. It is a still whisper within us.

Call it what you like—that doesn't matter, as its presence is universal and dwells within every single human being. Perhaps the simplest way to refer to it is the *"Voice for Love."*

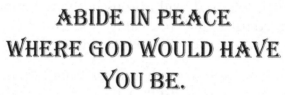

ABIDE IN PEACE
WHERE GOD WOULD HAVE
YOU BE.

T.558

Listening for this Voice requires some determination, intention, and patience, because there is another voice within us that can side track us. It's louder, full of fear, and reminds us of past experiences. If we're already upset, we can be sure we haven't listened to our true guidance system.

We aren't lost, however. We simply need to ask to see things differently. The *"Voice for Love"* will always give us new information that inspires loving action and restores us to peace.

WHEN
YOU ARE AFRAID,
BE STILL AND KNOW THAT
GOD IS REAL,
AND YOU ARE HIS BELOVED
SON (CHILD) IN
WHOM HE IS
WELL PLEASED.

T.55

The resulting shifts in emotions are the evidence of God's Love for us. This is a perfect time to pause and reflect on what just happened

We are meant to enjoy our lives. In *A Course in Miracles* it says that, "God's will for us is perfect happiness." If you are a parent or have chosen to care for a pet, you know that your first intention is for that "other" to experience goodness. It is the *"Love you Are"* that is inspiring this idea and will give you the strength to carry it out.

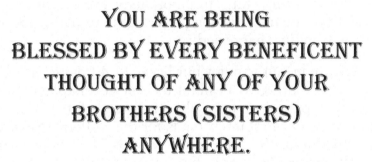

YOU ARE BEING
BLESSED BY EVERY BENEFICENT
THOUGHT OF ANY OF YOUR
BROTHERS (SISTERS)
ANYWHERE.

T.72

Now we have a template for the new Commandment: "Nurture the Awareness of Being Loved by God." We have begun the process of true self-reflection. By asking to see an upsetting experience differently, we have become willing to have greater peace and satisfaction in our lives. We have now captured a glimmer of the idea and the feeling that we are "Loved by God."

TO THINK LIKE GOD IS TO
SHARE HIS CERTAINTY OF WHAT
YOU ARE, AND TO CREATE
LIKE HIM IS TO
SHARE THE PERFECT LOVE
HE SHARES WITH
YOU.

T.113

Thus begins our journey of cashing in on all the "goodness" we have extended into the world through our willingness to follow the first Twelve Commandments of Moses and Jesus. We are blessed and it is time for us to accept these blessings, to become aware of how much our Creator Loves us, to minimize our shortcomings and bad decisions, to become aware of the Grace that is given us from our benevolent Creator. "We are loved more that we can possibly understand, for there is nothing in our human experience that resembles it ever so slightly," says *A Course In Miracles.*

THE STILL INFINITY
OF ENDLESS PEACE
SURROUNDS YOU GENTLY
IN ITS SOFT EMBRACE,
SO STRONG AND QUIET,
TRANQUIL IN THE MIGHT
OF ITS CREATOR,
NOTHING CAN INTRUDE
UPON THE SACRED SON (CHILD)
OF GOD WITHIN.

T.614

In the Psalms, we are told to "Make a joyful noise unto the Lord." The advice is to celebrate outwardly. It would be a way to say, "Thank You," which is totally appropriate.

But we haven't been told to nurture our feelings of *being loved by God*. Let's celebrate the awareness of how much we are loved by God whenever we experience what we label as "good."

THERE IS NOT
A MOMENT IN WHICH
HIS VOICE FAILS TO DIRECT
MY THOUGHTS, GUIDE MY ACTIONS
AND LEAD MY FEET.
I AM WALKING
STEADILY ON
TOWARDS
TRUTH.

WB.101

It's important that we get the feeling of being loved deep down in our bones. For too many of us, it's just an idea or thought someone has shared with us.

There are hundreds of things that happen in our lives every day that are the result of God's love for His creations. We build a consciousness of inner acceptance as we remember to say, "This is evidence that I am loved by God."

TO ACCEPT
YOUR LITTLENESS IS
ARROGANT, BECAUSE IT MEANS
THAT YOU BELIEVE YOUR
EVALUATION OF YOURSELF
IS TRUER THAN
GOD'S.

T.179

Can this practice make a difference in our lives? Is it possible to find peace at any chosen moment?

Have you ever been "in love?" In a romantic experience of love, especially where the experience is reciprocal, you know the magic that happens. Life is more joyous, your heart is overflowing with thoughts of goodness, you are inspired to bring gifts to the beloved, and conversation flows with dreams and possibilities. There is a feeling of oneness.

Yes, this practice changes us, because it cultivates the feeling of "being in love with God." Now the cycle is fulfilled; our hearts are one.

THE JOURNEY TO GOD IS
MERELY THE REAWAKENING OF THE
KNOWLEDGE OF WHERE YOU
ARE ALWAYS AND WHAT
YOU ARE FOREVER.

T.150

It's an interesting phenomenon that when we begin to register the feeling that *God loves us* we also have a feeling of *abundance*. Our human personality, which is derived from our past circumstances, training, and beliefs, operates from an entirely different feeling, the feeling of lack. It is responsible for addictions, the feeling we always need more of everything imaginable, and that we ourselves are not enough. We are actually operating out of an awareness of separation from our Source, God.

It isn't true; nevertheless, it becomes the motivation for all of the above behavior. Perhaps we can begin to understand why we have not been as happy as we could have been.

GOD'S
WILL FOR YOU IS
COMPLETE PEACE AND JOY;
UNLESS YOU EXPERIENCE ONLY
THIS, YOU MUST BE REFUSING
TO ACKNOWLEDGE
HIS WILL.

T.143

When Jesus told us to Love God, he understood that there is a law of correspondence at work. As our thoughts of appreciation and gratitude flow outward, our Creator responds by corresponding. The love we give returns to us multiplied and running over.

As it returns, we have to be ready to receive it. If our hearts are not open to this idea, we miss the beauty of our bountiful relationship with God.

YOU ARE
ALTOGETHER IRREPLACEABLE
IN THE MIND OF GOD.
NO ONE ELSE CAN FILL YOUR
PART IN IT, AND WHILE YOU LEAVE
YOUR PART EMPTY, YOUR
ETERNAL PLACE MERELY
AWAITS YOUR
RETURN.

T.179

We think that we must do everything alone. In Truth, we do nothing alone, for it is God energy that is always working. And when we consciously work with it we magnify the goodness that flows into our experience. There is a heightened feeling of union, oneness, support, and abundance. The circle of giving and receiving is complete. Joy fills our awareness.

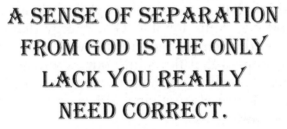

A SENSE OF SEPARATION
FROM GOD IS THE ONLY
LACK YOU REALLY
NEED CORRECT.

T.14

It is from joy that life becomes richer, more exciting, and productive for everyone.

The gifts we have are not to be hoarded by us. God gave them to be shared, and when we listen to the *"Voice for Love"* we will find ourselves lifted to new heights of consciousness where Spirit can inspire and instruct us for the good of all.

GLORY
IS GOD'S GIFT
TO YOU, BECAUSE THAT
IS WHAT HE IS.
SEE THIS GLORY EVERYWHERE
TO REMEMBER WHAT
YOU ARE.

T.143

Are you willing to open your "Joy" center? It is really quite natural once you have the idea in mind. Most of us have never given it much thought.

But an undisciplined mind leads us blindly into temptation, precisely what the Ten Commandments and the Two Commandments advise against.

Instead, let's remember the Thirteenth Commandment and nurture the *feeling* that God loves us.

THE
GRACE OF GOD
RESTS GENTLY
ON FORGIVING EYES,
AND EVERYTHING THEY
LOOK UPON SPEAKS
OF HIM TO THE BEHOLDER.
HE CAN SEE NO EVIL,
NOTHING IN THE
WORLD TO FEAR, AND NO ONE
WHO IS DIFFERENT
FROM HIMSELF.

T.529

Once we become aware at a conscious level of how much we are loved, we will find ourselves living almost completely free from fear. Our inner guidance system, the *"Voice for Love,"* will gently move us away from old behaviors that brought unpleasant experiences in the past. The *"Voice for Love"* will remind us that appreciating the goodness that comes into our lives is a way of remembering also, that God loves us!

Feeling loved inspires us to extend love, and the cycle begins all over again. Life becomes much sweeter.

EACH DAY,
EACH HOUR, EVERY INSTANT
I AM CHOOSING WHAT
I WANT TO LOOK UPON,
THE SOUNDS I WANT TO HEAR,
THE WITNESSES TO
WHAT I WANT TO BE
TRUTH FOR ME.

WB.432

Every day we face challenges in our relationships, at work, with our finances, health, or a number of other things. We usually deal with such earthly matters by relying on conventional wisdom or our past experiences.

As we embrace and experience the feeling of being loved by God, though, we awaken a different part of our self, the Holy aspect, the Spiritual aspect, the True Self. It is actually our Joy or Love Center.

THE HOLY SPIRIT'S
TEACHING TAKES ONLY ONE
DIRECTION AND HAS ONLY ONE
GOAL.
HIS DIRECTION IS FREEDOM
AND HIS GOAL IS
GOD.

T.141

This is what it means to be created in the "image and likeness of our Creator." To abide in this awareness, is to live from our greatest potential with which we have been created.

It's not just for some of us, but for all of us. God's love for us inspires the beauty of creation to be extended outward, so that all may see His glory constantly.

We are equipped to live in a peaceful world where everyone has enough with plenty to share. It hasn't happened yet, though, because we haven't yet fully embraced, understood, and exercised our greatest capabilities.

YOUR HOLINESS REVERSES
ALL THE LAWS OF THE WORLD.
IT IS BEYOND EVERY RESTRICTION
OF TIME, SPACE,
DISTANCE, AND LIMITS
OF ANY KIND.

WB.58

With the Thirteenth Commandment, the world as we know it can change. There are pockets of society throughout the planet where this awareness is already flourishing. We don't have to travel abroad to have this experience, though. We can cultivate it right here in our own homes.

To do so is an act of healing. Broken or worn relationships can be mended as we look through the eyes of love, guided by the *"Voice for Love"* from within. All it takes is a little determination, willingness, and faith that one's own actions can really make a difference.

THERE IS A PLACE
IN YOU WHERE
THERE IS PERFECT PEACE.
THERE IS A PLACE IN YOU WHERE
NOTHING IS IMPOSSIBLE.
THERE IS A PLACE IN YOU WHERE
THE STRENGTH OF
GOD ABIDES.

WB.76

We are amazed at what has become common through science and technology in the last century. We can also become amazed at the peace we begin to feel when we rest in the assurance that God loves us and that we truly have an awareness of this, deep down in our souls. We can look at a sunset, the miracle of a new day, hear the sound of a bird, and feel the Presence of God's love right where we are.

WHAT YOU SEE REFLECTS YOUR
THINKING,
AND YOUR THINKING BUT
REFLECTS YOUR CHOICE
OF WHAT YOU
WANT TO SEE.

WB.237

Are we used to becoming still, or is our every moment occupied with an endless "to do" list?

Are we worthy of taking care of ourselves? We know what happens when we don't.

These little moments of stillness and inner listening are investments in our divine well being.

THINK BUT AN
INSTANT ON THIS; YOU
CAN BEHOLD THE HOLINESS GOD
GAVE HIS SON(CHILD)
AND NEVER NEED YOU THINK
THAT THERE IS SOMETHING
ELSE FOR YOU TO SEE.

T.444

With daily times of quiet reflection, we can shift our awareness, or our inner conversation, away from problems, concerns, and challenges, and fly away to that Holy place within where the Presence of love abides.

One might initiate the experience by remembering an event or being with a person in which there was a great feeling of love. Contemplating this activity, we can begin to focus on our heart space, noticing what is happening to our feeling nature.

WHERE GOD
IS, THERE ARE YOU.
SUCH IS THE TRUTH.
T.290

After a few moments, we can watch the loving situation begin to fade until we are simply aware of the feeling of love in our hearts. Here comes the opportunity for the "shift." We can imagine that this feeling is God loving US!

We know what it feels like to extend love outward, but let's begin to receive the feeling back, magnifying it as our focus endures.

When we enter into the stillness on a regular basis, the effect is cumulative. We become anchored in the "knowingness" that we are loved by God.

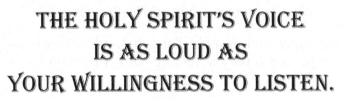

THE HOLY SPIRIT'S VOICE
IS AS LOUD AS
YOUR WILLINGNESS TO LISTEN.
T.157

In his book, *Proof of Heaven,* Eben Alexander, M.D., recites the message he understood from the seven days he was in a coma: "You are loved and cherished."

With The Thirteenth Commandment I see an awakening within the consciousness of humanity. By moving from a feeling of scarcity to a feeling of abundance, our whole motivation for actions shifts. Nurtured by an awareness of the Presence of love, we move from inspiration on High, or the *"Voice for Love."*

YOU CANNOT
UNDERSTAND HOW MUCH
YOUR FATHER LOVES YOU,
FOR THERE IS NO PARALLEL
IN YOUR
EXPERIENCE OF THE WORLD
TO HELP YOU
UNDERSTAND IT.

T.281

This Voice always has the good of the whole in mind and backs up the thoughts or ideas with the means for bringing them into fruition. Just as our grandparents and other ancestors had no idea of the electronic devices that we take for granted in our age, we are on the cusp of a new age of living in peace and prosperity.

We have the tools at hand and the shift is happening. It doesn't take a huge leap of mental ability to step into a new way of life, we simply move from gratitude for something "out there" to a deeper feeling of being loved by God in "here."

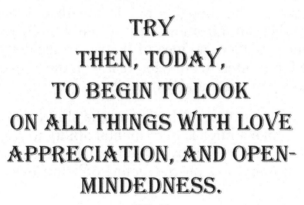

TRY
THEN, TODAY,
TO BEGIN TO LOOK
ON ALL THINGS WITH LOVE
APPRECIATION, AND OPEN-
MINDEDNESS.
WB.45

We can know, as all humanity, that the good we experience is always the result of our Creator's love for us. We can pray to be sensitive to this activity, thus building our awareness of unity, oneness, and love itself!

To follow the Ten Commandments of Moses as well as the Two Commandments Jesus reminded us of, has been a way to shepherd society into behavior that replicates the great love in which we were created.

WHEN A MIND
HAS ONLY LIGHT,
IT KNOWS ONLY LIGHT.
ITS OWN RADIANCE SHINES ALL
AROUND IT, AND EXTENDS OUT
INTO THE DARKNESS OF OTHER
MINDS
TRANSFORMING THEM INTO
MAJESTY.

T.137

It's not until we become personally awake to this loving presence that we can fully own the limitless gifts that have been bestowed upon us. We have come full circle, and what we feel, we can more easily share.

When we feel our Creator's love for us we are fueled from the inside, and it just naturally spills out from us.

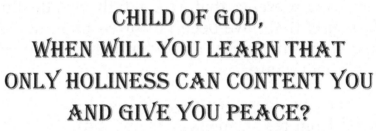

CHILD OF GOD,
WHEN WILL YOU LEARN THAT
ONLY HOLINESS CAN CONTENT YOU
AND GIVE YOU PEACE?

T.308

A Course in Miracles tells us, "In this world you can become a spotless mirror, in which the Holiness of your Creator shines forth from you to all around you. You can reflect Heaven here." T.292

Are you willing to move forward now? We stand at the apex of generations who have sought a "better way." Inspired leaders in all areas of life have known that Love is the answer. With the Thirteenth Commandment clearly stated, perhaps we have found the way at last!

God has blessed us on our journey.

♥

ABOUT THE AUTHOR

Rev. Frances Lancaster lives in Hillsboro, Oregon. She is an independent minister lecturing, teaching, writing and facilitating study groups. She has a degree in Education from Washington State University and has written curriculum for both adults and children to use in Metaphysical churches. She has served in the leadership capacity of both local and international New Thought organizations. Her passion centers on helping people learn to create fulfilling and productive lives as they serve one another through conscious connection with our Creator's inspiration and guidance.

WISEWOMAN PRESS

Books by Frances B. Lancaster

- *Abundance Now*
- *Happiness Now*

Books by Emma Curtis Hopkins

- *Resume*
- *Gospel Series*
- *Class Lessons of 1888*
- *Self Treatments including Radiant I Am*
- *High Mysticism*
- *Genesis Series 1894*
- *Esoteric Philosophy in Spiritual Science*
- *Drops of Gold Journal*
- *Judgment Series*
- *Bible Interpretations: Series I, thru XVII*

Books by Ruth L. Miller

- *Unveiling Your Hidden Power: Emma Curtis Hopkins' Metaphysics for the 21st Century*
- *Coming into Freedom: Emily Cady's Lessons in Truth for the 21st Century*
- *150 Years of Healing: The Founders and Science of New Thought*
- *Power Beyond Magic: Ernest Holmes Biography*
- *Power to Heal: Emma Curtis Hopkins Biography*
- *The Power of Unity: Charles Fillmore Biography*
- *Power of Thought: Phineas P. Quimby Biography*
- *The Power of Insight: Thomas Troward Biography*
- *The Power of the Self: Ralph Waldo Emerson Biography*
- *Uncommon Prayer*
- *Spiritual Success*
- *Finding the Path*

www.wisewomanpress.com

Made in the USA
Coppell, TX
17 November 2019